MW01119062

ON ONE FOOT ™

Written by Mitchell G. Bard, Ph.D.
American-Israeli Cooperative Enterprise

Published by BE, Inc.
To order additional copies call 1-310-364-0909
or Email info@ononefootbook.com

ISBN 0-9740070-0-5

PURPOSE OF ON ONE FOOT

It can happen in a restaurant with friends, at a party, or on your way to class: someone offers a statement, a fact, a position, a logical argument about human suffering in the Middle East, which is, at the same time, a condemnation of the State of Israel.

Suddenly, where once you felt comfortable with your sense of justice, you find it difficult to respond. Is it true? Where you once thought Israel stood for justice and democracy, is it possible that Israel has now emerged as a Goliathan oppressor of a defenseless, downtrodden people, who are struggling for their human rights?

How do you respond? Are you quiet because you do not want to reveal your own confusion? Do you feel an instinct that makes you want to argue a point you are not equipped to make? Do you suddenly feel like an outsider, perhaps even unwelcome, among those with whom you thought you shared common values?

The purpose of this book is to present accessible and balanced information to help you respond to complex, competing and often emotional statements about Israel. These discussions can be the most difficult when held with friends, family, even parts of your own inner dialogue, as you attempt to find justice within the events you see in the media every day. It is a difficult task; there is tremendous pain on all sides. This book is a limited reference tool. We encourage you to do more research. Read all you can on every side of the issues and draw your own conclusions.

The name of this book is drawn from the famous Talmudic story of Hillel the Elder (end of 1st century BCE), who is confronted by a man demanding to learn Torah. The man wants the knowledge, wants it fast, and demands to have it while "standing on one foot." Hillel responds, "What is hateful to you, do not do to your fellow man. This is the entire Torah, all of it; the rest is commentary."

In our hyperspeed world, we too need to get some fast learning, often while we are on one foot, struggling for balance, seeking the truth.

Thomas K. Barad

INTRODUCTION

HOW TO USE THIS BOOK

Two easy ways:

The book is organized under eight subject sections. First, you may scan the table of contents for the phrase that reflects the most frequently heard statements, accusations or claims within a subject. Refer to the corresponding page for three brief responses and an overview.

Second, ON ONE FOOT can be read through as a reference guide, to help you achieve an overall understanding of the confusing often mythologized rhetoric floating around campus, or wherever else you may travel.

Finally, we recognize that the complex issues relating to the Middle East cannot be comprehensively addressed in such a short volume. Further study is heartily recommended. A bibliography and a "web-ography" for further research has been provided. We especially recommend *Myths and Facts: A Guide to the Arab-Israeli Conflict* for more specific responses to common myths. See also the Jewish Virtual Library (www.JewishVirtualLibrary.org) for a comprehensive encyclopedia of Jewish history and culture.

ABOUT THE AUTHOR

Mitchell Bard is the Executive Director of the nonprofit AMERICAN-ISRAELI COOPERATIVE ENTERPRISE (AICE) and a foreign policy analyst who lectures frequently on U.S.-Middle East policy. Dr. Bard is also the director of the Jewish Virtual Library (www.JewishVirtualLibrary.org), the world's most comprehensive online encyclopedia of Jewish history and culture. For three years he was the editor of the *Near East Report*, the American Israel Public Affairs Committee's (AIPAC) weekly newsletter on U.S. Middle East policy. Prior to working at AIPAC, Dr. Bard served as a senior analyst in the polling division of the 1988 Bush campaign. Dr. Bard has appeared on Fox News, MSNBC and other local and national television and radio outlets. His work has been published in academic journals, magazines and major newspapers. Dr. Bard is the author of 16 books. He holds a Ph.D. in political science from UCLA and a master's degree in public policy from

Berkeley. He received his B.A. in economics from the University of California at Santa Barbara.

ADDITIONAL MATERIAL CONTRIBUTED BY:

Thomas K. Barad	Barad Entertainment, Inc. Los Angeles, CA
Rabbi Elliot N. Dorff, Ph.D.	Distinguished Professor of Philosophy at the University of Judaism, Los Angeles, California
Ellen Frankel, Ph.D.	CEO and Editor-in-Chief of The Jewish Publication Society, Philadelphia, Pennsylvania
Rabbi Daniel Landes	Director and Rosh Yeshivah, Pardes Institute of Jewish Studies, Jerusalem
Lori Hope Lefkovitz, Ph.D.	Academic Director, Kolot: The Center for Jewish Women's and Gender Studies, Wyncote, Pennsylvania
Rabbi David Wolpe	Sinai Temple, Los Angeles, California
Efraim Zuroff, Ph.D.	Director, Simon Wiesenthal Center, Israel

TABLE OF CONTENTS

SUBJECT: ROOTS OF CONFLICT

SUBJECT: PEACE

TABLE OF CONTENTS

SUBJECT: DISPUTED TERRITORIES & SETTLEMENTS

TABLE OF CONTENTS

SUBJECT: HUMAN RIGHTS

SUBJECT: REFUGEES

TABLE OF CONTENTS

TABLE OF CONTENTS

ROOTS OF CONFLICT

Who is wise? One who learns from every other human being....

Who is honorable? One who honors every other human being....

Mishna Avot, Chapter 4

(D.L.)

STATEMENT:

"Jews have no right to a state in 'Palestine.'"

ONE FOOT RESPONSES:

- A common misperception is that the Jews, after being forced into the Diaspora by the Romans in the year 70 C.E., suddenly, 1,800 years later, returned to Palestine demanding their country back. The Jewish people have maintained ties to their historic homeland for more than 3,700 years. Independent Jewish states existed for more than 400 years.

- An independent Jewish state would be 3,000 years old today if not for foreign conquerors. Even after most Jews were exiled, small Jewish communities remained in the Land of Israel. Jews have lived there continuously for the last 2,000 years. Modern Israel developed the land from a largely uninhabited wasteland filled with malarial swamps into a thriving high-tech Western society.

- Jews have fought and died to win independence in their homeland. They are connected to the Land of Israel by both faith and history. The international community granted political sovereignty in Palestine to the Jewish people. By contrast, there has never been an independent Palestinian state.

HISTORY:

Israel's international "birth certificate" was validated by Jewish statehood in the Land of Israel in Biblical times; an uninterrupted Jewish presence from the time of Joshua onward; the Balfour Declaration of 1917; the League of Nations Mandate, which incorporated the Balfour Declaration; the United Nations partition resolution of 1947; Israel's admission to the UN in 1949; the recognition of Israel by most other states; and, most of all, the society created by Israel's people in decades of thriving, dynamic national existence.

STATEMENT:

"Jews stole Arab land."

ONE FOOT RESPONSES:

- The Jews bought land from Arabs who were happy to sell it, including the Arab mayors of Gaza, Jerusalem, and Jaffa. Analyses of land purchases from 1880 to 1948 show that 73% of Jewish plots were purchased from large landowners.

- In 1931, the British offered new plots to any Arabs who had been "dispossessed." Out of more than 3,000 applications, British officials found that 80% were false claims and not landless Arabs. This left only about 600 landless Arabs, 100 of whom accepted the Government land offer

- In 1937 the British Peel Commission found that Arab complaints about Jewish land acquisition were baseless. It pointed out that "much of the land now carrying orange groves was sand dunes or swamp and uncultivated when it was purchased." To the extent there was a land shortage, the Commission found that it was "due less to the amount of land acquired by Jews than to the increase in the Arab population."

HISTORY:

Jews avoided purchasing land in areas where Arabs might be displaced. They sought land that was largely uncultivated, swampy, cheap and, most important, without tenants. It was only after the Jews had bought all of the available uncultivated land that they began to purchase cultivated land. According to British statistics, more than 70% of the land in what would become Israel was not owned by Arab farmers, it belonged to the mandatory government. Those lands reverted to Israeli control after the departure of the British. Nearly 9% of the land was owned by Jews and about 3% by Arabs who became citizens of Israel. That means only about 18% belonged to Arabs who left the country before and after the Arab invasion of Israel.

STATEMENT:

"Palestine was always an Arab country."

ONE FOOT RESPONSES:

- The Twelve Tribes of Israel formed the first constitutional monarchy in the Land of Israel in about 1000 B.C.E. The second king, David, first made Jerusalem the nation's capital. Although Israel eventually was split into two separate Israelite kingdoms, Jewish independence under the monarchy lasted for more than 400 years.

- The Arab connection to Palestine dates only to the Muslim invasions of the seventh century. Palestine was never an exclusively Arab country. No independent Arab or Palestinian state ever existed in Palestine.

- When the distinguished Arab-American historian, Princeton University Prof. Philip Hitti, testified against partition before the Anglo-American Committee in 1946, he said: "There is no such thing as 'Palestine' in history." Most Palestinian Arabs, including the original PLO chairman, believed Palestine was part of southern Syria.

HISTORY:

The term "Palestine" is believed to be derived from the Philistines, an Aegean people who, in the 12th Century B.C.E., settled along the Mediterranean coastal plain of what is now Israel and the Gaza Strip. In the second century C.E., after crushing the last Jewish revolt, the Romans first applied the name Palaestina to Judea (the southern portion of what is now called the West Bank) in an attempt to minimize Jewish identification with the land of Israel. The Arabic word "Filastin" is derived from this Latin name.

STATEMENT:

"The Palestinians are descendants of the Canaanites and were in Palestine long before the Jews."

ONE FOOT RESPONSES:

- The Canaanites disappeared from the face of the earth three millennia ago, and no one knows if any of their descendants survived or, if they did, who they would be. Palestinian claims to be related to them are a recent phenomenon and contrary to historical evidence.

- Over the last 2,000 years, there have been massive invasions that killed off most of the local people (e.g., the Crusades), migrations, the plague, and other man-made or natural disasters. The entire local population was replaced many times over. During the British mandate alone, more than 100,000 Arabs emigrated from neighboring countries and are today considered Palestinians.

- Even the Palestinians themselves have acknowledged that their association with the region came long after the Jews. In testimony before the Anglo-American Committee in 1946, for example, the Palestinian spokesmen claimed a connection of only 1,000 years, and even that assertion is dubious.

HISTORY:

The Jewish people have a connection to the Land of Israel that dates back more than 3,700 years. They created a monarchy that dominated parts of the area for more than 400 years. Even after the defeat of the monarchy and the end of Jewish independence, a Jewish presence remained in the Land of Israel throughout the centuries preceding the reestablishment of the Jewish state in 1948. While, at best, the Palestinians can claim a connection to the area following the conquest of Muhammad's followers in the 7th century, no serious historian questions the Jewish connection to the land or relation to the ancient Hebrews.

5

SUBJECT: ROOTS OF CONFLICT

STATEMENT:

"Zionism is racism; anti–Zionism is different from anti–Semitism."

ONE FOOT RESPONSES:

- Zionism is the national liberation movement of the Jewish people, which holds that Jews, like any other nation, are entitled to a homeland. This has nothing whatsoever to do with race. Israel's Law of Return grants automatic citizenship to Jews, but non-Jews are also eligible to become citizens under normalization procedures similar to those in other countries.

- Israel's citizens include Jews from more than 100 countries, including dark-skinned Jews from Ethiopia, Yemen, and India. Palestinian Arabs and other non-Jews may also become citizens of Israel. In fact, Muslim and Christian Arabs, Druze, Baha'is, Circassians and other ethnic groups represent more than 20% of Israel's population.

- The UN repealed its infamous Zionism equals racism resolution in 1991. The 1975 UN resolution was part of the Soviet-Arab Cold War anti-Israel campaign. Almost all the former non-Arab supporters of the resolution have apologized and changed their positions.

HISTORY:

Zionism emerged in the 19th century as Theodor Herzl and other Jewish visionaries came to the conclusion that anti-Semitism could not be eradicated and that Jews could not escape persecution by assimilation. They believed the best solution was the creation of a state in the home-land of the Jewish people – the Land of Israel. This homeland ensures Jewish security, providing a safe haven to protect Jews from a future Inquisition or Holocaust. For all but a small minority, Zionism is an integral part of being Jewish. Martin Luther King Jr., one of the most vehement critics of racism, understood this, so when he was approached by a student who attacked Zionism during a 1968 appearance at Harvard, he responded that "when people criticize Zionists, they mean Jews. You're talking anti-Semitism."

6

STATEMENT:

"Criticizing Israel doesn't make you anti-Semitic."

ONE FOOT RESPONSES:

- It is true that criticizing Israel doesn't necessarily make you anti-Semitic. The question is the intent of the critic.

- Legitimate critics accept Israel's right to exist whereas anti-Semites do not. Anti-Semites use double standards when they criticize Israel; for example, denying Israelis the right to pursue their legitimate claims while encouraging the Palestinians to do so.

- Anti-Semites deny Israel alone the right to defend itself, and ignore Jewish victims, while blaming Israel for pursuing their murderers.

HISTORY:

Criticism of Israeli policy is perfectly legitimate. In fact, the most vociferous critics of Israel are Israelis themselves who use their freedom of speech to express their concerns every day. You need only look at any Israeli news paper and you will find the pages filled with articles denouncing particular government policies. Israelis want to improve their society; anti-Semites do not have the interests of Israel's citizens—Jews or non-Jews—at heart. Anti-Semites are interested in first delegitimizing the state and then, ultimately, destroying Israel. There is nothing Israel could do to satisfy them. And don't fall for the line that Arabs as "Semites" cannot possibly be anti-Semitic. This is a semantic distortion that ignores the reality of Arab discrimination and hostility toward Jews. Arabs, like any other people, can indeed be anti-Semitic, and the word has been accepted and under-stood to mean hatred of the Jewish people.

PEACE

"Seek peace and pursue it." (Psalms 34:15)

Jewish law does not order you to run after or pursue the other commandments, but only to fulfill them on the appropriate occasion. But peace you must seek in your own place and pursue it even to other places as well.

Jerusalem Talmud, Pe'ah 1:1.   (E.D.)

STATEMENT:

"The Oslo peace process failed because of Israel's actions."

ONE FOOT RESPONSES:

- The Oslo process was predicated on promises Yasser Arafat made to Prime Minister Rabin in a September 1993 letter. In it he "recognizes the right of the State of Israel to exist," "renounces the use of terrorism," and pledges that outstanding issues "will be resolved through negotiations." He reneged on all of these commitments either in word or deed or both.

- Since the 1993 Oslo agreement, Israel has traded land — nearly all the Gaza Strip and more than 40% of the West Bank — in expectation of peace, but the Palestinians have not reciprocated. Had the Palestinians fulfilled their obligations, they would have a state today in 100% of Gaza and more than 90% of the West Bank.

- At summit meetings with President Clinton and Arafat in 2000, Prime Minister Barak offered the Palestinians a contiguous state on 95% of the West Bank and 100% of Gaza, with a capital in east Jerusalem. He offered to dismantle more than 100 settlements as well. Arafat rejected the deal and made no counterproposal. This convinced most Israelis no concessions would satisfy him.

HISTORY:

Israel expected Yasser Arafat to be like Egyptian President Anwar Sadat and adhere to his formal commitment to peace. As in the Egyptian negotiations, Israel offered a gradual withdrawal from territory in exchange for peace, but unlike the Egyptians, the Palestinians did not fulfill their treaty obligations. Instead of negotiating their disputes, they turned to violence. While Israelis have accepted the Palestinian demand for a Palestinian state next to Israel, the Palestinians have remained committed to a state replacing Israel.

9

STATEMENT:

"The Palestinian Authority fulfilled its commitment to prevent violence by arresting terrorists and confiscating illegal weapons."

ONE FOOT RESPONSES:

- No one other than the Palestinian police is permitted to have lethal weapons. Despite repeated promises, no effort has been made to collect the illegal weapons. On the contrary, the PA has been actively stockpiling them, as was evident when Israel captured the *Karine-A* ship filled with 50 tons of weapons and explosives for the PA. This is a serious violation of the agreements signed with Israel, one that provokes distrust and threatens Israeli security.

- According to the State Department, the Palestinians have reneged on their pledge not to use violence; have failed to confiscate illegal weapons and protect holy sites; and have continued to incite the Palestinian public, including children, to use violence.

- The PA has failed to take adequate measures to prevent terrorism. While many terrorists have been apprehended, they are usually released shortly afterward, and many of them subsequently murdered Jewish men, women, and children. Furthermore, organizations directly under Yasser Arafat's control have increasingly engaged in terrorist attacks.

HISTORY:

Israel recognized the need for the Palestinians to have a police force to keep internal peace, but the agreement was very specific about the number of officers and the weapons they could possess. There are more police than allowed, more weapons than agreed to, and the police have been more active in attacks against Israelis than in preventing them. Arafat also renounced terror, a prerequisite to Israel's decision to negotiate with him after Oslo, but he has not arrested the leaders of the terror groups and taken any serious measures to prevent the murder of Israelis. Instead, he is instigating violence.

10

"The Palestinians teach their children about Israel and encourage coexistence with Israeli Jews."

ONE FOOT RESPONSES:

- The PA has violated its treaty commitments to abstain from incitement and hostile propaganda. The Palestinians indoctrinate their children with anti-Semitic stereotypes, anti-Israel propaganda and other materials designed to promote hostility and hatred. Summer camps teach Palestinian children how to resist the Israelis and that the greatest glory is to be a martyr.

- Palestinian textbooks make little or no mention of Jews or the centuries-old Jewish communities of Palestine. Israel is not mentioned and does not appear on maps. References to Jews are usually stereotypical and related in a negative way to their opposition to Muhammad and refusal to convert to Islam.

- Palestinian television also encourages hatred for Jews and the perpetration of violence against them. In one song on a children's show, young children sing about wanting to become "suicide warriors" and taking up machine guns against Israelis. Another song has the refrain, "When I wander into Jerusalem, I will become a suicide bomber." TV commercials tell children to drop their toys, pick up rocks, and do battle with Israel.

HISTORY:

One of the keys to future peace in the region is the education of children. Unfortunately, the Palestinians have chosen to indoctrinate their youth with hatred of Jews, to encourage martyrdom, and glorify terrorism. The Palestinian authorities also try to convince children that Israel is out to kill them by all sorts of devious methods. For example, the Palestinian daily newspaper falsely claimed Israeli aircraft were dropping poison candy in the Gaza Strip. These teachings violate the letter and spirit of the peace agreements.

STATEMENT:

"Israeli textbooks don't recognize the Palestinians or encourage coexistence with them."

ONE FOOT RESPONSES:

• Israeli textbooks are oriented toward peace and tolerance. The Palestinians are accepted as Palestinians. Islam and Arab culture are referred to with respect. Islamic holy places are discussed along with Jewish ones. Stereotypes are avoided to educate against prejudice.

• The Arab-Israeli conflict is factually described as an ongoing conflict between two national entities over the same territory. Both the Arab and Israeli sides are presented.

• The content of the peace treaties between Israel and Egypt and Jordan is detailed, along with the implications of those agreements. Agreements with the Palestinians are discussed as well, and the atlas used in Israeli schools shows the Palestinian Authority.

HISTORY:

The best hope for the future is that Israeli and Arab children will grow up with a greater understanding and tolerance of one another. Unfortunately, the textbooks in Arab countries, and the Palestinian Authority, in particular, do not promote coexistence. They typically do not recognize Israel or the Jewish connection to Israel. By contrast, young Jews are educated about the history and culture of their neighbors and tolerance toward others is promoted.

12

STATEMENT:

"Arafat rejected Barak's proposals in 2000 because they did not offer the Palestinians a viable state."

ONE FOOT RESPONSES:

- Israel offered to create a Palestinian state that was contiguous, and not a series of cantons. Barak offered to withdraw from 95% of the West Bank and 100% of the Gaza Strip, and to dismantle more than 100 settlements.

- Barak made previously unthinkable concessions on Jerusalem, agreeing that Arab neighborhoods of East Jerusalem would become the capital of the new state and the Palestinians would have "religious sovereignty" over the Temple Mount.

- The proposal guaranteed the right of Palestinian refugees to return to the Palestinian state and reparations from a $30 billion international fund

for resettlement in other countries. Israel also agreed to allow the Palestinians access to water desalinated in its territory to ensure them adequate water.

HISTORY:

Arafat was asked by Barak to accept Israeli sovereignty over the parts of the Western Wall religiously significant to Jews, and three early warning stations in the Jordan valley, which Israel would withdraw from after six years. Most important, however, Arafat was expected to agree that the conflict was over at the end of the negotiations. This was the deal breaker. Arafat was not willing to end the conflict. The consensus of Mideast analysts — that Israel offered generous concessions and that Arafat rejected them to pursue a violent insurrection — was undisputed for more than a year before the Palestinians recognized they had to counter the widespread view that Arafat was the obstacle to peace. They subsequently manufactured excuses for why Arafat failed to say "yes" to a proposal that would have established a Palestinian state. Had the terms of the proposal really been the problem, all Arafat had to do was offer a counterproposal. He never did.

13

STATEMENT:

"The Golan Heights has no strategic significance for Israel."

ONE FOOT RESPONSES:

- Syria — deterred by an IDF presence within artillery range of Damascus — has kept the Golan quiet since 1974. But Syria provides a haven and supports numerous terrorist groups that attack Israel from Lebanon and other countries. In addition, Syria still deploys hundreds of thousands of troops — as much as 75% of its army — on the Israeli front near the Heights.

- From the western Golan, it is only about 60 miles — without major terrain obstacles — to Haifa and Acre, Israel's industrial heartland. The Golan — rising from 400 to 1700 feet — overlooks the Hula Valley, Israel's richest agricultural area. In the hands of a friendly neighbor, the escarpment has little military importance. If controlled by a hostile country, however, the Golan has the potential to again become a strategic nightmare for Israel.

- For Israel, relinquishing the Golan to a hostile Syria without adequate security arrangements could jeopardize its early-warning system against surprise attack. No withdrawal from the Golan Heights is possible without a credible guarantee of peace from Syria accompanied by security arrangements to insure the Heights do not become a threat to Israel.

HISTORY:

Between 1948 and 1967, Syria controlled the Golan Heights and used it as a military stronghold from which its troops sniped at Israeli civilians in the Hula Valley below, forcing children living on kibbutzim to sleep in bomb shelters. In addition, during this period, many roads in northern Israel could be crossed only after being cleared by mine-detection vehicles. Israel repeatedly, and unsuccessfully, protested the Syrian bombardments to the UN, but nothing was done to stop Syria's aggression.

SUBJECT: PEACE

STATEMENT:

"Israel has rejected Syrian offers to trade peace for the Golan Heights."

ONE FOOT RESPONSES:

- Since attacking Israel in 1973 and losing the Golan Heights, Syria has insisted that Israel completely withdraw from the Golan Heights before discussing what Syria might do in return. Syria has never agreed to make peace with Israel, even if Israel returned the entire Golan. Israel has been equally adamant that it will not give up any territory without knowing what Syria is prepared to concede.

- Israel's willingness to trade some or all of the Golan is dependent on Syria's agreement to sign an agreement that would bring about an end to the state of war Syria says exists between them.

- Besides military security, a key to peace with Syria is the normalization

of relations between the two countries. But this cannot happen as long as Syria sponsors terrorism and allows Damascus to serve as a haven for terrorist groups.

HISTORY:

Israel repeatedly tried to negotiate directly with then-Syrian President Hafez Assad, but Assad would never agree to meet with any Israeli leader. Although Israel long held that it would be too dangerous to give up the Golan Heights, Israeli prime ministers, beginning with Yitzhak Rabin expressed a willingness to compromise. Assad would not budge, however, insisting that Israel give Syria access to the shore of the Kinneret (Israel's foremost water reservoir), and died without reaching any agreement with Israel. When Assad's son Bashar came to power, Israelis were hopeful that Syrian policy might change and that negotiations could be resumed. To date, however, the younger Assad has been unwilling to discuss peace with Israel. Absent dramatic changes in Syria's policy, Israel's security will require the retention of military control over the Golan Heights.

STATEMENT:

"A Palestinian state will pose no danger to Israel."

ONE FOOT RESPONSES:

- A Palestinian state could become dominated by Islamic extremists and serve as a staging area for terrorists. Hamas and Islamic Jihad say they will never accept the existence of Israel.

- A Palestinian state could serve as a forward base in a future war for Arab nations that have refused to make peace with Israel. The West Bank now represents a valuable defensive asset that deters Arab foes from attacking Israel along an eastern front.

- Palestinians say a West Bank state is only the first stage in their plan to destroy Israel. "Our ultimate goal is the liberation of all historic Palestine from the River to the Sea," said the late "moderate" Faisal Husseini, "We distinguish the strategic, long-term goals from the political phased goals" (*Al-Arabi*, – June 24, 2001).

HISTORY:

Though reconciled to the creation of a Palestinian state, and hopeful that it will coexist peacefully, Israelis still see such an entity as a threat to their security. Even after returning much of the West Bank and Gaza Strip, and allowing the Palestinians to govern themselves, terrorism against Israelis has continued. Consequently, Israelis are reluctant to give up additional territory for a Palestinian state. If the Palestinians were content to have a state in the West Bank and Gaza, the prospects for peace would be bright, since Prime Minister Barak offered just that in 2000; however, they have consistently held out for much more. Their actions and rhetoric since Oslo suggests the dream of returning to their homes in Jaffa, Haifa and elsewhere has not died. A Palestinian state may be created beside Israel, but cannot replace Israel.

STATEMENT:

"The Saudi plan offers Israel full peace in exchange for withdrawal from the 'occupied' territories."

ONE FOOT RESPONSES:

- Israel has no obligation to withdraw to the 1967 borders as the plan requires. In fact, the UN Security Council explicitly rejected the basic premise of the Saudi proposal in the debate over Resolution 242 when it refused to adopt the Arab proposal to require that Israel withdraw from "all" the territories.

- The plan calls for Israel to withdraw from the Golan Heights. The Israeli government has offered to withdraw from most, if not all the Golan in exchange for a peace agreement; however, Syria has refused to trade peace for the land.

- The Arab demand that Israel accept the establishment of a Palestinian State in the West Bank and Gaza with East Jerusalem as its capital has been part of the negotiations since Oslo. Israeli leaders have accepted the idea of creating a Palestinian state in part of the disputed territories, but Palestinian violence has prevented a final settlement from being negotiated.

HISTORY:

Most of the Arab League nations have no reason to remain at war with Israel since Israel holds none of their territory and has sought peace with them for the last 54 years. Several members of the League had already begun to normalize relations with Israel before the latest outbreak of violence, and their principal critic was Saudi Arabia. Even though the Saudi initiative had many unacceptable elements, Israel still welcomed it as a starting point for negotiations. First, however, the Saudis and other Arab League members would have to be prepared to negotiate directly with Israel, but they refuse to do so.

STATEMENT:

"The 'Bush Plan' calls for Israel to withdraw to the 1967 borders and to freeze settlement construction."

ONE FOOT RESPONSES:

- President George W. Bush laid out a road map for advancing the Israeli-Palestinian peace process that is consistent with the policies of the last several Israeli prime ministers. Bush rightly focuses on three elements that are prerequisites to peace: the removal of Arafat as leader of the Palestinian Authority, the reform of the PA, and an end to violence.

- The Bush Plan places demands on Israel, but the Palestinian terror must first stop, and the PA must begin to reform before Israel is obligated to act. Bush called for Israel to withdraw its troops from PA territories, not to the 1967 border. Israel has also agreed to the Mitchell Plan and its call for freezing settlement activity, but the implementation of Mitchell first requires a cessation of violence, and that plan also includes a number of other recommendations requiring Palestinian action.

- President Bush has reinforced Israel's long-held view that a Palestinian state "will never be created by terror." He envisions a Palestinian state side by side with Israel, both living in peace and security. This is a vision shared by Israel's leaders as well.

HISTORY:

President Bush's main innovation in his June 24, 2002, speech was to turn the establishment of a Palestinian state from an unconditional certainty to a conditioned possibility. He ended his speech with the Biblical injunction that when given the choice between life and death, one should choose life. This is the view of the Jewish people and the citizens of Israel. It is not the view of suicide bombers and those who glorify them. When the Palestinians share Israelis' commitment to choosing life, the prospects for peace will be brighter.

18

STATEMENT:

"Yasser Arafat is the democratically elected leader of the Palestinian people and Israel must negotiate with him."

ONE FOOT RESPONSES:

- Palestinians have the right to select their own leaders, but both Israel and the United States also have the right to decide which leaders they are prepared to recognize and negotiate with. Israel cannot be expected to negotiate with someone who conducts a terror campaign against its citizens. Every Arab leader who has recognized Israel and been prepared to make peace has gotten both land and peace.

- The Palestinian Authority is a corrupt dictatorship run by a terrorist who was "elected" in a sham election in 1996, and whose term was supposed to be over long ago. He clings to power through intimidation and violence. Only true democratic elections monitored by international observers with multiple candidates can bring representative leadership to the Palestinians.

- When the Palestinians democratically elect a leader who is prepared to recognize Israel's right to exist, end violence, and negotiate peace, they will find a willing and eager partner in Israel.

HISTORY:

As the only democracy in the region, one which allows women to vote and even pro-PLO Israeli Arabs to serve in its parliament, Israel respects democratically elected leaders. Israelis, like Americans, believe that democracies do not make war on each other, so it is in Israel's interest to see that the Palestinians develop democratic institutions. To date, however, the history of the Palestinians is one in which leaders are determined by bullets, not ballots.

STATEMENT:

"Ariel Sharon does not want peace and no deal is possible as long as he is Prime Minister."

ONE FOOT RESPONSES:

- The only way to tell if Sharon is really against peace is to test him through negotiations. So long as the Palestinians keep up their terrorist attacks, no Israeli prime minister can negotiate and offer compromises.

- While Sharon was once fiercely opposed to the creation of a Palestinian state, as Prime Minister he has endorsed the idea, in opposition to members of his own party. Since taking office, Sharon has repeatedly offered to negotiate with the Palestinians on condition they end the violence.

- Sharon has spent most of his life as a soldier and public servant trying to bring peace to his nation.

HISTORY:

Ariel Sharon has been demonized by the Arabs and caricatured by the media, which often insists on referring to him as the "right-wing" or "hardline" Prime Minister, appellations rarely affixed to any other foreign leaders. In 1978, at a crucial moment in the Camp David negotiations, Egyptian President Anwar Sadat insisted that all Israeli settlements in the Sinai be dismantled. Prime Minister Menachem Begin called Sharon and asked if he should give up the settlements; Sharon not only advised him to do so, but ultimately was the one who implemented the decision to remove the settlers, some by force. Sharon can and will make peace if he has a willing and courageous partner, as Begin did.

20

STATEMENT:

"The American government is unfairly biased toward Israel."

ONE FOOT RESPONSES:

- Historically, the U.S. has long sought friendly relations with Arab leaders primarily because of the need to protect our oil supplies. The U.S. has sold billions of dollars worth of arms to Arab states, and poured billions of dollars of economic and military assistance into the region. Today, America considers Jordan, Saudi Arabia, Morocco, Egypt, and the Gulf sheikdoms close friends.

- American presidents have often criticized Israel and taken actions against Israel when they believed it was in the U.S. interest. Dwight Eisenhower threatened to withhold aid from Israel. Harry Truman embargoed arms to Israel in 1948 as did Lyndon Johnson in 1967. Ronald Reagan suspended a strategic cooperation agreement. Bill Clinton and George W. Bush have used waivers to avoid moving the U.S. embassy to Jerusalem.

- The U.S. gives Israel the arms to have a qualitative edge, but the U.S. has also armed Arab nations, providing sophisticated missiles, tanks and aircraft to Jordan, Morocco, Egypt, Saudi Arabia and the Gulf states. The U.S. gives Israel a large amount of foreign aid, but also rewards Arab states that have made peace with Israel, giving money to Egypt, Jordan, and, even before the Oslo accords, the Palestinians.

HISTORY:

Israel is a country surrounded by potential threats and with large numbers of immigrants to absorb. While Israel's enemies have numerous countries helping them, Israel relies primarily on the United States for assistance. Like the U.S., Israel is a democracy and a nation of immigrants, and the two nations share the same values; therefore, it makes sense that the U.S. supports Israel. However, the U.S. has always looked out first for its own interests and has not hesitated to both criticize Israel and help Arab nations when it deems it necessary.

STATEMENT:

"Media coverage of the Middle East is balanced."

ONE FOOT RESPONSES:

- Press coverage is distorted in part because of the difference in the availability of information. Israel is a democracy with a free press, while the media in the Arab/Islamic world is strictly controlled by totalitarian governments.

- Few correspondents have a background in Middle East history or speak the regional languages. Journalists are more familiar with the largely Western Israeli culture than the culturally distant Muslim societies. News agencies often rely on biased locals, especially in the Palestinian Authority, to gather news for them.

- The price of access to dictators and terrorists in the Arab world is often to present their side of the story, usually without any objectivity. Reporters are sometimes intimidated or blackmailed. Journalists are usually

escorted to see what the dictator wants them to see or they are followed. Case in point, an Associated Press cameraman's life was threatened to prevent AP from airing his film of Palestinians celebrating the September 11 terror attacks at a rally in Nablus.

HISTORY:

One reason Americans are so knowledgeable about Israel is the extent of coverage. American news organizations usually have more correspondents in Israel than in any country except Great Britain. The amount of attention Israel receives is also related to the fact that the largest Jewish population in the world is in the United States and that Israel greatly concerns American Jews. Non-Jews are also fascinated by the Holy Land and are concerned about the impact of the region's conflicts on U.S. interests. The biased casting of Israel as "Goliath" and the Palestinians as "David" inaccurately implies that Israelis are bullies and Palestinians are victims. Americans also tend to have a double-standard about the Jews, expecting more from them than from other peoples.

DISPUTED TERRITORIES & SETTLEMENTS

Jewish tradition teaches that we should all carry in our pockets two slips of paper: on one, the statement that we are but dust and to dust we shall return. On the other, that it was for our sake that the world was created. The first teaching instills within us the humility we need to bring peace to the world. The second teaching dares us to bring about its redemption.   (E.F.)

SUBJECT: DISPUTED TERRITORIES & SETTLEMENTS

STATEMENT:

"Israel illegally seized and occupied Palestinian land in 1948 and 1967."

ONE FOOT RESPONSES:

- Nearly 80% of the historic land of Palestine, and the Jewish National Home as defined by the League of Nations, was severed by the British in 1922 to create Jordan. The UN partitioned the remaining 20% of Palestine into two states. The 1948 war began after the Arabs refused to accept partition and attacked Israel.

- The 1967 war was a response to Arab terrorist attacks and threats of war, the massing of Egyptian and Syrian troops near the Israeli border, and Egypt's illegal closure of the Straits of Tiran to Israeli ships. After the war, Israel offered to trade land for peace, and has withdrawn from more than 90% of the territories it won in the war, including all of the Sinai, nearly all of the Gaza Strip, more than 40% of the West Bank, and part of the Golan Heights.

- In 1967, Israel did not capture the West Bank from any legitimate sovereign because there was none. The territory had been conquered by Transjordan in 1948, and illegally occupied until 1967. It was never a Palestinian state.

HISTORY:

Jewish settlements were expressly recognized as legitimate in the League of Nations Mandate for Palestine, which provided for the establishment of a Jewish state in the Jewish people's ancient homeland. Some settlements, such as in Hebron, existed throughout the centuries of Ottoman rule, while others were established prior to the establishment of the State of Israel. Many present-day Israeli settlements were established on sites that were home to Jewish communities in previous generations, long before 1948. Israeli settlements were established under the supervision of Israel's Supreme Court to ensure that no communities were established on private Arab land, and that no Arab inhabitants were displaced.

24

STATEMENT:

"Israeli settlements are illegal."

ONE FOOT RESPONSES:

- A country acting in self-defense may seize and control territory when necessary to protect itself, and may require, as a condition for its withdrawal, security measures to ensure that its citizens are not menaced again from that territory.

- UN Security Council Resolution 242 gives Israel a legal right to administer the territories it won in the 1967 war until peace is achieved.

- Palestinians may live in Israel; in fact, 20% of the Israeli population is non-Jewish. Immigration laws may place limits on who may live in a country, but are discriminatory if they do so on the basis of race or religion. If someone said that Jews should not be allowed to live in your hometown, they would be denounced as an anti-Semite and yet Palestinians insist Jews have no right to live in the West Bank.

HISTORY:

While Israelis agree that Jews have the right to live anywhere, many question whether they should. Many Israelis have concerns about the expansion of settlements. Some consider them provocative. Others worry that the settlers are particularly vulnerable to Palestinian terrorist attacks. To defend the settlements, large numbers of soldiers are deployed who would otherwise be training and preparing for a possible future conflict with an Arab army. Some Israelis also object to the amount of money that goes to communities beyond the Green Line and special subsidies that have been provided to make housing there more affordable. Still others feel the settlers are providing a first line of defense and developing land that rightfully belongs to Israel.

SUBJECT: DISPUTED TERRITORIES & SETTLEMENTS

ONE FOOT RESPONSES:

- Jews have lived in the West Bank and Gaza Strip since ancient times. The only time Jews have been prohibited from living in the territories in recent decades was during Jordan's illegal rule from 1948 to 1967.

- When Israel made peace with Egypt, it dismantled the Jewish settlements in the Sinai. If Israel withdraws toward the 1967 border unilaterally, or as part of a political settlement, settlers will face several scenarios: remain in the territories, expulsion from their homes, or voluntary resettlement in Israel.

- The impediment to peace is not the existence of settlements, it is the Palestinians' unwillingness to accept a state next to Israel instead of one replacing Israel.

HISTORY:

From 1948-67, when Jews were forbidden to live on the West Bank, the Arabs refused to make peace with Israel. From 1967-77, the Labor Party established only a few strategic settlements, and the Arabs remained at war. After his election in 1977, Prime Minister Menachem Begin increased the number of settlements, but Egypt made peace with Israel. Later, Begin froze settlement building for three months, hoping the gesture would entice other Arabs to join the Camp David peace process. But none would. In 1994, Jordan signed a peace agreement with Israel, and settlements were not an issue. Yasser Arafat signed the Oslo agreements without any requirement that settlements be removed. In 2000, Prime Minister Barak offered to dismantle settlements to make peace with the Palestinians, but Arafat rejected the deal. The settlements remain a matter for negotiation as part of the final status talks that have been forestalled by Palestinian violence.

SUBJECT: DISPUTED TERRITORIES & SETTLEMENTS

STATEMENT:

"Israel 'occupies' the West Bank and the violence can only end when the occupation ends."

ONE FOOT RESPONSES:

- Occupation is foreign control of an area that was under the previous sovereignty of another state. The West Bank was never Palestinian territory. By rejecting Arab demands that Israel be required to withdraw from all the territories won in 1967, UN Resolution 242 acknowledged that Israel was entitled to claim at least part of these lands for new defensible borders.

- After the Oslo accords, Israel transferred virtually all civilian authority over Palestinians in the West Bank and Gaza to the Palestinian Authority. Israel retained the power to control its own external security and that of its citizens, but 98% of the Palestinian population in these territories came under the PA's authority.

- The more accurate description of the territories in Judea and Samaria is "disputed" territories. Palestinian terrorists are not "resisting occupation," they are committing what Amnesty International labels "crimes against humanity."

HISTORY:

The PLO was formed to fight Israel in 1964, before Israel controlled the West Bank. "Occupation" could not have been the issue then. Additionally, even though Israel has withdrawn from most of the Gaza Strip and nearly half the West Bank, and offered to withdraw from100% of Gaza and 95% of the West Bank, Palestinian violence has only increased. Consequently, Israel has had to reassert control over certain areas to rout terrorists operating with the permission of the PA. Israel has said it will withdraw from these areas when the Palestinians root out the terrorists. The Palestinians must resolve their complaints against Israel through negotiations, and not by violence.

STATEMENT:

"Hundreds of Israeli soldiers are refusing to serve in the territories because Israel's policies there are unjust."

ONE FOOT RESPONSES:

- A handful of "refuseniks" became celebrities because Israelis rarely refuse to serve their country. Only 0.08% of Israeli reservists were "refuseniks." Meanwhile, the media ignored the fact that Israelis who were not obligated to report because they were too old, had disabilities, or were otherwise excused from service, volunteered to go to the territories during Operation Defensive Shield, bringing the reporting rate to more than 100%.

- In a democracy, such as Israel, people may protest their government's policies, but the voices of a minority do not carry more weight than the majority. A Tel Aviv University poll showed that nearly 80% of the public rejected the "refuseniks'" argument.

- Soldiers can't decide which legal orders they wish to carry out. If the refuseniks' principles were adopted, other soldiers might take the exact opposite position and refuse to carry out orders the refuseniks supported. Israeli security depends on soldiers' obedience to the elected officials of the nation and the apolitical nature of the security system.

HISTORY:

The soldiers raised important issues about the treatment of Palestinians that are taken seriously by the Israeli public and government, but their actions were also politically motivated and not mere acts of conscience. Israel's democracy gives them other outlets to pursue their political agenda, namely creating a new political movement or using an existing one to change Israeli policy. While their actions come with a real cost to them individually, and should be respected, the refuseniks' views are of small import compared to the 99.02% of reservists who are serving at the potential cost of their lives.

HUMAN RIGHTS

Hillel the Elder (2nd century BCE) revolutionized Judaism with his strong humanistic/individualistic approach:

A gentile approached Shammai and said, "I will become a Jew, on condition that you teach me the whole Torah while I stand on one foot." Shammai chased him off with a measuring-stick. The gentile then approached Hillel, who told him, "What is hateful to you, do not to others! That is the whole Torah: The rest is only commentary - go learn it!"

(Talmud, Shabbat 31a) (D.L.)

STATEMENT:

"Israel discriminates against its Arab citizens."

ONE FOOT RESPONSES:

- Roughly 20% of the Israeli population are non-Jews. The sole legal distinction between Jewish and Arab citizens of Israel is that the latter are not required to serve in the Israeli army. This is to spare Arab citizens the need to take up arms against their brethren. Druze and Circassians do serve, and Bedouins and other Arabs have volunteered for military duty.

- Arabs in Israel have equal voting rights; in fact, it is one of the few places in the Middle East where Arab women may vote. Israeli Arabs have also held various government posts and are represented in Israel's parliament. Arabic, like Hebrew, is an official language in Israel.

- Palestinians are more welcome in Israel, where they enjoy full political rights and economic opportunity, than in most Arab countries, where they aren't granted citizenship. Jordan is the only Arab state that offers Palestinians citizenship.

HISTORY:

Israel committed itself in its declaration of independence to protect the rights of all its citizens and has been a model society in terms of tolerance toward people from all faiths and backgrounds. Still, it would be misleading to suggest that this promise has been completely fulfilled. As in all other countries in the world, discrimination does occur, and there are economic and social gaps between Israeli Jews and Arabs. Israelis are the first to admit their society is not perfect, and greater efforts have been made in recent years to redress the grievances of Israeli Arabs.

STATEMENT:

"Israel's treatment of Palestinians resembles the treatment of blacks in apartheid South Africa."

ONE FOOT RESPONSES:

- Under apartheid, black South Africans could not vote and were not citizens of the country in which they formed the overwhelming majority of the population. Within Israel, Jews are a majority, but the Arab minority are full citizens with voting rights and representation in the government.

- Israel's parliament has several Arab members representing a number of different parties. There are no restrictions on them, even though they are often outspokenly critical of the government. Arabs have served in the Cabinet, in the foreign service, and on the Supreme Court. Black South Africans had no such opportunities.

- "We do not want to create a situation like that which exists in South Africa where the whites are the owners and rulers, and the blacks are the workers," David Ben-Gurion told a Palestinian nationalist. "If we do not do all kinds of work, easy and hard, skilled and unskilled, if we become merely landlords, then this will not be our homeland."

HISTORY:

The situation of Palestinians in the territories is different from those who are Israeli citizens. The security requirements of the nation, and a violent insurrection in the territories, forced Israel to impose restrictions on Arab residents of the West Bank and Gaza Strip that are not necessary inside Israel's pre-1967 borders. If Israel were to give Palestinians in the territories full citizenship, it would mean the territories had been annexed. No Israeli government has been prepared to take that step, nor is that what the Palestinians want. Today, 98% of Palestinians in the territories are under the jurisdiction of the Palestinian Authority and they are entitled to vote in PA elections. Their other rights are determined by the dictatorial policy of Yasser Arafat.

STATEMENT:

"American universities should divest from companies that do business in Israel to force an end to Israeli 'occupation' and human rights abuses."

ONE FOOT RESPONSES:

- The word "peace" does not appear in divestment petitions, which makes clear the intent is not to resolve the conflict but to delegitimize Israel. Petitioners blame Israel for the lack of peace and demand that it make unilateral concessions without requiring anything of the Palestinians, not even the cessation of terrorism.

- Divestment advocates ignore Israel's efforts during the Oslo peace process, and at the summit meetings with President Clinton, to reach historic compromises with the Palestinians that would have created a Palestinian state.

- Advocates call on Israel to negotiate on the basis of UN Security Council Resolution 242. Israel has done so since 1967; it is the Palestinians who ignore the resolution's clause that every state in the area has the "right to live in peace within secure and recognized boundaries free from threats or acts of force."

HISTORY:

Peace in the Middle East will come only from direct negotiations between the parties, and only after the Arab states recognize Israel's right to exist, and the Palestinians and other Arabs cease their support of terror. American universities cannot help through misguided divestment campaigns that unfairly single out Israel as the source of conflict in the region. Proponents hope to tar Israel with an association with apartheid South Africa, an offensive comparison that ignores the fact that all Israeli citizens are equal under the law. The divestment campaign against South Africa was specifically directed at companies that were using that country's racist laws to their advantage. In Israel no such racist laws exist; moreover, companies doing business there adhere to the same standards of equal working rights that are applied in the United States.

STATEMENT:

"Israel uses checkpoints to humiliate Palestinians and imposes curfews as collective punishment."

ONE FOOT RESPONSES:

- Checkpoints were set up to ensure the safety of Israeli citizens in the territories, protecting them from terrorism on the roads. The passage of Palestinians from the territories into Israel was limited to prevent the spillover of violence and terrorism into Israeli cities. Commercial goods, food, medicine, ambulances, and medical crews continue to circulate freely, hampered only by continuing attacks.

- Curfews are imposed after repeated terrorist attacks force Israel to monitor the movements of prospective terrorists and limit their ability to enter Israel. They are not designed to punish the Palestinian people; curfews are necessary security measures to defend Israeli citizens.

- Israel wants open borders with its Palestinian neighbors; however, the unrelenting terrorist attacks on its civilian population have forced Israel to defend itself. Israel is in a war and must sometimes take harsh measures, such as the imposition of curfews, but these steps are taken according to the laws of the state and are subject to judicial review.

HISTORY:

Although there have been abuses of human rights, as in any society, these are the exceptions, and not the rule. These are investigated and, where warranted, condemned and the violators punished. Israeli law demands that Palestinians be treated humanely, even those suspected of terrorism or other crimes. Barriers such as checkpoints are set up not to humiliate, but to ensure the security of Israeli citizens. Once the Palestinians end their campaign of terror, Israel will not need checkpoints and other security measures. Israel has repeatedly offered to end such measures when the Palestinians prove they will prevent terrorism, but each time Israel has relaxed these precautions, violence has escalated against Israeli civilians.

STATEMENT:

"Israel is pursuing a policy of genocide toward the Palestinians that is comparable to the Nazis' treatment of the Jews."

ONE FOOT RESPONSES:

- The Nazis were engaged in the systematic extermination of every Jew in Europe. Israelis have no desire to harm the Palestinian people. Israel seeks peace with the Palestinians.

- More than one million Arabs live as free and equal citizens in Israel. Of the Palestinians in the territories, 98% live under the civil administration of the Palestinian Authority. The only people threatened by Israel are Palestinians who pursue terror against Israeli citizens.

- While Israel sometimes employs harsh measures against Palestinians in the territories to protect Israeli citizens—Jews and non-Jews—from the incessant campaign of terror waged by the PA and Islamic radicals, there is no plan to persecute, exterminate, or expel the Palestinian people. Even during terror attacks, Israel has continually provided medical assistance and support to save Palestinian lives.

HISTORY:

This is perhaps the most odious claim made by Israel's detractors. Hitler's "Final Solution" was designed to exterminate every Jew. The extermination of the Jews had no justification and was considered an equal part of the German war effort. Israel has sought accommodation with the Palestinians for nearly a century, and repeatedly offered concessions for the sake of peace. The Palestinian population has increased exponentially, in part because of the benefits of living beside the Jews and under Israel's prosperous democracy. If anyone warrants comparison with the Nazis, it is the Arabs, who use Nazi imagery in the press, have made *Mein Kampf* a bestseller, collaborated with Hitler, and have pursued their own campaign to destroy the Jewish people.

STATEMENT:

"Israel was responsible for the killing of innocent Palestinian refugees at Sabra and Shatila in Lebanon in 1982."

ONE FOOT RESPONSES:

- The Lebanese Christian Phalangist militia was responsible for the killing of an estimated 460-800 people in the two refugee camps. Israeli troops allowed the Phalangists to enter them to root out terrorist cells believed located there. The Phalangists decided to also avenge past murders of Christians by Palestinians.

- Israel had allowed the Phalange to enter the camps as part of a plan to transfer authority to the Lebanese, and accepted responsibility for that decision. The Israeli public was outraged when it learned what happened and demanded an investigation. Subsequently, a commission of inquiry found Israeli forces indirectly responsible for the massacre, and Defense Minister Ariel Sharon was dismissed.

- While 300,000 Israelis demonstrated in Israel to protest the killings, little or no reaction occurred in the Arab world. There was a major international outcry against Israel, but not the Phalangists, who actually perpetrated the crime.

HISTORY:

The incident at Sabra and Shatila was a tragedy, but it was committed at the hands of the Phalangists, not the Israelis. It would have never happened had Palestinian terrorists not attacked Israel and provoked a war, and it probably would not have occurred had Palestinians not previously murdered large numbers of Lebanese Christians. Israel responded democratically, with an investigation, and punishment of those deemed "indirectly responsible." By contrast, there were no UN condemnations or investigations of the May 1985 massacre of 635 Palestinian refugees perpetrated by Muslim militiamen in the Shatila and Burj-el Barajneh camps or the October 1990 Syrian attack on Christian-controlled areas of Lebanon in which 700 Christians were killed.

STATEMENT:

"Jews who lived in Islamic countries were well-treated by the Muslims."

- At times, Jews in Muslim lands lived in relative peace and thrived culturally and economically. When Jews were perceived as having achieved too comfortable a position in Islamic society, anti-Semitism would surface, often with devastating results. Mass murders of Jews in Arab lands occurred at various times and places throughout the history of the Muslim empire.

ONE FOOT RESPONSES:

- The Golden Age of equal rights was a myth. Jews were generally viewed with contempt by their Muslim neighbors; peaceful coexistence between the two groups involved the subordination and degradation of the Jews. In the ninth century, the Caliph in Baghdad designated a yellow badge for Jews, setting a precedent that would be followed centuries later in Nazi Germany.

- The negative Muslim attitude toward Jews is reflected in various verses throughout the Koran, the holy book of the Islamic faith. According to the Koran, the Jews try to introduce corruption, have always been disobedient, and are enemies of Allah, the Prophet and the angels.

HISTORY:

The 1947 UN debate over the partition of Palestine highlighted the precarious position of Jews in Muslim lands. The Syrian delegate, Faris el-Khouri, warned: "Unless the Palestine problem is settled, we shall have difficulty in protecting and safeguarding the Jews in the Arab world." More than a thousand Jews were killed in anti-Jewish rioting during the 1940's in Iraq, Libya, Egypt, Syria and Yemen. This helped trigger the mass exodus of Jews from Muslim countries.

36

STATEMENT:

"Arabs cannot be anti-Semitic as they are themselves Semites."

ONE FOOT RESPONSES:

- The term "anti-Semite" was coined in Germany in 1879 to refer to the anti-Jewish manifestations of the period and to give Jew-hatred a more scientific sounding name.

- "Anti-Semitism" has been accepted and understood to mean hatred of the Jewish people. Dictionaries define the term as: "Theory, action, or practice directed against the Jews" and "Hostility towards Jews as a religious or racial minority group, often accompanied by social, economic and political discrimination."

- The claim that Arabs, as "Semites," cannot be anti-Semitic is a semantic distortion that ignores the reality of Arab discrimination and hostility toward Jews. Arabs, like any other people, can indeed be anti-Semitic.

HISTORY:

While Jewish communities in Islamic countries fared better overall than those in Christian lands in Europe, Jews were no strangers to persecution and humiliation among the Arabs. Today, virulent anti-Semitism is common throughout the Arab world, evident by blood libels (where Jews are said to sacrifice gentile children and use their blood to make unleavened bread) and Nazi-like cartoons published in government-controlled newspapers, and the popularity of anti-Semitic tracts such as *Mein Kampf* and the *Protocols of the Elders of Zion*.

REFUGEES

Whoever destroys a single soul is considered as if he had destroyed the whole world; and whoever saves one soul is considered as if he had saved the whole world.

Mishna Sanhedrin, Albeck edition (D.L.)

STATEMENT:

"Israel expelled all the Palestinians in 1948."

ONE FOOT RESPONSES:

- The Arab exodus began immediately following the announcement of the UN partition resolution when roughly 30,000 wealthy Arabs who anticipated the upcoming war fled to neighboring Arab countries to await its end.

- Arab leaders urged the Palestinian Arabs to leave their homes and convinced them their armies would destroy Israel and then they could return to their homes as well as those of the Jews.

- Contemporary press reports of major battles conspicuously fail to mention any forcible expulsion by the Jewish forces. The Arabs are usually described as "fleeing" or "evacuating" their homes. In a handful of extraordinary instances, small numbers of Arabs were expelled. Most left to avoid being caught in the crossfire of the war.

HISTORY:

Had the Arabs accepted the 1947 UN resolution, not a single Palestinian would have become a refugee. An independent Arab state would now exist beside Israel. The refugee problem was due to a combination of flight due to fear of war, the orders of Arab leaders, and, in a handful of instances, expulsions by Israel; thus, the responsibility for the refugee problem lies primarily with the Arabs. The 150,000 Palestinian Arabs who chose to stay in their homes became full citizens of Israel. Ironically, today, thousands of Palestinians who are now under Palestinian Authority rule are fleeing the West Bank and Gaza Strip.

STATEMENT:

"The Palestinians were the only refugees from the Arab-Israeli conflict."

ONE FOOT RESPONSES:

- The number of Jews fleeing Arab countries for Israel in the years following Israel's independence was roughly equal to the number of Arabs leaving Israel.

- The situation of Jews in Arab countries had long been precarious. During the 1947 UN debates, Arab leaders threatened them. For example, Egypt's delegate told the General Assembly: "The lives of one million Jews in Muslim countries would be jeopardized by partition."

- Many Jews were allowed to take little more than the shirts on their backs. Little is heard about them because they did not remain refugees for long. Of the 820,000

Jewish refugees, 586,000 were resettled in Israel at great expense, and without any offer of compensation from the Arab governments who confiscated their possessions. Any agreement to compensate the Palestinian refugees should also include Arab compensation for Jewish refugees.

HISTORY:

While the Jewish refugees were welcomed in Israel, the Arab governments put the Palestinian refugees in camps and, with the exception of Jordan, denied them citizenship. The contrast between the reception of Jewish and Palestinian refugees is even starker considering the difference in cultural and geographic dislocation experienced by the two groups. Most Jewish refugees traveled hundreds—and some traveled thousands—of miles to a tiny country whose inhabitants spoke a different language. Most Arab refugees never left Palestine at all; they traveled a few miles to the other side of the truce line, remaining inside the vast Arab nation that they were part of linguistically, culturally and ethnically.

STATEMENT:

"UN Resolution 194 requires Israel to repatriate all the Palestinian refugees."

ONE FOOT RESPONSES:

- UN Resolution 194 (adopted December 1948) says that "refugees wishing to return to their homes and live at peace with their neighbors should be permitted to do so." The refugees have never expressed a willingness to live in peace with Israel and their return would mean the end of Israel.

- Resolution 194 also calls for "the repatriation, resettlement and economic and social rehabilitation of refugees and payment of compensation...." The UN recognized that Israel could not be expected to repatriate a hostile population that might endanger its security.

- Previous refugee problems in world history have been resolved through resettlement in new or neighboring countries. Israel considered the settlement of the refugee issue a negotiable part of an overall peace settlement and thought the Arab states would resettle the majority and some compromise on the remainder could be worked out in negotiations. The Arabs refused to compromise in 1949, just as they did in 1947. In fact, they unanimously rejected Resolution 194.

HISTORY:

The Arab states have prevented the resettlement of the Palestinian refugees. Jordan is the only Arab state that grants citizenship to Palestinians. The Palestinian Authority has received billions of dollars in aid, but has not moved the refugees out of camps under its control and into permanent housing. Meanwhile, Israel has allowed thousands of refugees to return and compensated thousands more. No Israeli government will allow the nearly four million Palestinians to move to Israel because it would mean Palestinians would likely outnumber Jews in the future, and the Jewish state would cease to exist.

JERUSALEM

He who cannot change the very fabric of his thought will never be able to change reality, and will never, therefore, make any progress.

--Anwar Sadat (88)

For centuries, philosophers have debated whether reality exists outside our heads or within them. If the world is only our own private dream, we need not change others—for they are only the figments of our own imagination. But if we do in fact share a physical universe with other people, then we need to imagine ourselves into their dreams as well. (E.F.)

STATEMENT:

"Jerusalem is an Arab city and therefore the rightful capital of a Palestinian state."

ONE FOOT RESPONSES:

- Jews have been living in Jerusalem continuously for nearly two millennia. They have constituted the largest single group of inhabitants there since the 1840's. Ever since King David made Jerusalem the capital of Israel more than 3,000 years ago, the city has played a central role in Jewish existence.

- The fact that Jerusalem is disputed, or that it is of importance to people other than Israeli Jews, does not mean the city belongs to others.

- Jerusalem was never the capital of any Arab entity. In fact, it was a backwater for most of Arab history.

Jerusalem never served as a provincial capital under Muslim rule, nor was it ever a Muslim cultural center. During the 19 years Jordan ruled the Old City no mention was ever made of making Jerusalem the capital of a Palestinian state.

HISTORY:

Jerusalem is mentioned more than 700 times in the Jewish Bible. It is not mentioned once in the Koran. The Western Wall in the Old City—the last remaining wall of the ancient Jewish Temple complex, the holiest site in Judaism—is the object of Jewish veneration and the focus of Jewish prayer. Three times a day, for thousands of years, Jews have prayed "To Jerusalem, your city, shall we return with joy," and have repeated the Psalmist's oath: "If I forget you, O Jerusalem, let my right hand forget her cunning." For Jews, the entire city is sacred, but Muslims revere a site—the Dome of the Rock—not the city.

STATEMENT:

"Israel limits freedom of religion in Jerusalem and denies Muslims and Christians access to their holy sites."

ONE FOOT RESPONSES:

- After the 1967 war, Israel abolished all the discriminatory laws promulgated by Jordan. "Whoever does anything that is likely to violate the freedom of access of the members of the various religions to the places sacred to them," Israeli law stipulates, is "liable to imprisonment for a term of five years."

- Israel entrusted administration of the holy places to their respective religious authorities. Thus, for example, the Muslim Waqf has responsibility for the mosques on the Temple Mount.

- Since 1967, hundreds of thousands of Muslims and Christians—many from Arab countries that remain in a state of war with Israel—have come to Jerusalem to see their holy places. Arab leaders are free to visit Jerusalem to pray if they wish to, just as Egyptian President Anwar Sadat did at the al-Aksa mosque.

HISTORY:

Former U.S. President Jimmy Carter acknowledged that religious freedom has been enhanced under Israeli rule. There is "no doubt" that Israel did a better job safeguarding access to the city's holy places than did Jordan. "There is unimpeded access today," Carter noted. "There wasn't from 1948-67."

44

STATEMENT:

"The Temple Mount has always been a Muslim holy place and Judaism has no connection to the site."

ONE FOOT RESPONSES:

- The Temple Mount is the site of both the First and Second Temples, which were the centers of Jewish religious and social life for more than a thousand years until the Second Temple's destruction by the Romans in 70 C.E.

- The Koran—the holy book of Islam—describes King Solomon's construction of the First Temple (34:13) and recounts the destruction of the First and Second Temples (17:7).

- The supreme Muslim body in Jerusalem during the British Mandate published a book that said the Temple Mount's "identity with the site of Solomon's Temple is beyond dispute. This, too, is the spot, according to universal belief, on which David built there an altar unto the Lord, and offered burnt offerings and peace offerings."

HISTORY:

The Jewish connection to the Temple Mount dates back more than 3,000 years and is rooted in tradition and history. When Abraham bound his son Isaac upon an altar as a sacrifice to God, tradition says he did so atop Mount Moriah, today's Temple Mount. Solomon built his Temple on this spot and, after being destroyed by the Babylonians in 586 B.C.E., it was rebuilt. After the destruction of the Second Temple in 70 C.E., control of the Temple Mount passed through several conquering powers. It was during the early period of Muslim control, in 691, that the gold-topped Dome of the Rock was built on the site of the ancient Jewish Temples.

45

STATEMENT:

"Jerusalem should be an international city, not the Israeli capital."

ONE FOOT RESPONSES:

- Ever since King David made Jerusalem the capital of Israel more than 3,000 years ago, the city has been central to Jewish existence. The Western Wall in the Old City — the last remaining wall of the mount on which the Jewish Temple stood — is the holiest Jewish site.

- Israel is the only government that has given people of all faiths access to their holy sites. From 1948 to 1967, Jordan denied Israelis access to the Western Wall and to the cemetery on the Mount of Olives. They desecrated Jewish cemeteries and synagogues, and passed discriminatory laws against Christians. Israel, in contrast, entrusted administration of the holy places to their respective religious authorities and passed laws safeguarding every religion's holy sites.

- There is no precedent for an international city. The closest thing was postwar Berlin when the four powers shared control of the city, and that experiment was a disaster. Additionally, no international group could be entrusted to protect the freedoms Israel already guarantees.

HISTORY:

In 1995, Congress passed legislation declaring that Jerusalem should be recognized as the undivided, eternal capital of Israel and required that the U.S. embassy in Israel be established in Jerusalem, although presidential waivers have subsequently delayed the move.

VIOLENCE

Even though our enemies treat us with the utmost cruelty - they murder us, crucify us and burn us alive - we are still commanded, when we have the upper hand, to treat them with compassion.

Sifri Deuteronomy

This was written over two thousand years ago and it is just as relevant today. Note, however, how different this is from "turning the other cheek."   (D.L.)

STATEMENT:

"Ariel Sharon's visit to the Temple Mount in September 2000 provoked the 'al-Aksa intifada.'"

ONE FOOT RESPONSES:

- The Mitchell Commission appointed to investigate the causes of violence concluded in its May 4, 2001, report: "The Sharon visit did not cause the 'Al-Aksa Intifada.'"

- Imad Faluji, the Palestinian Authority Communications Minister, admitted months after Sharon's visit that the violence had been planned far in advance. "It [the uprising] had been planned since Chairman Arafat's return from Camp David, when he turned the tables on the former U.S. president and rejected the American conditions."

- Israel's Internal Security Minister permitted Sharon to go to the Temple Mount—Judaism's holiest place—only after receiving assurances from the Palestinian security chief that no problems would arise if Sharon did not enter the mosques. Sharon stayed away from the mosques and his visit ended peacefully, with serious rioting erupting more than 24 hours later.

HISTORY:

The Temple Mount is a holy place for Jews, and they have long been able to visit when Muslims are not at prayers. Given Sharon's image among Palestinians, his decision to visit may have been provocative, but still would not have justified violence, which anyway began before his brief pilgrimage, and has now continued for more than two years since his 34-minute visit.

STATEMENT:

"Palestinians resort to terror because they are desperate, impoverished and frustrated."

ONE FOOT RESPONSES:

- Terrorism is not the only response available to the Palestinians' discontentment. Palestinians do have an option for improving their situation — it is called negotiations.

- Many peoples and leaders have found alternatives to violence to pursue their political goals. For example, the Palestinians could choose the nonviolent path taken by Martin Luther King or Mahatma Gandhi. Unfortunately, they have chosen to pursue a war of terror instead of a process for peace.

- Terrorism is not the product of freedom fighters, but rather of totalitarianism. Adolf Hitler, Josef Stalin, Saddam Hussein, and other despots killed civilians in pursuit of a "cause." Totalitarianism annihilates life, art, free speech, individual rights, and hope.

HISTORY:

Many Palestinians live in poverty, see the future as hopeless, and are frustrated. None of these are excuses for engaging in terrorism. Terrorism has little to do with poverty. In fact, many terrorists are not poor, desperate people at all. The world's most wanted terrorist, Osama bin Laden, for example, is a Saudi millionaire. Terrorism is not Israel's fault. It is not the result of "occupation." The Palestinian leadership has made a conscious decision to eschew negotiations and pursue violence. Israel has proven time and again a willingness to trade land for peace, but it can never concede land for terror.

STATEMENT:

"Members of Islamic Jihad, Hamas and the PFLP are 'freedom fighters' and not terrorists."

ONE FOOT RESPONSES:

- Nowhere else in the world is the murder of innocent men, women and children considered a "legitimate form of resistance." The long list of heinous crimes by Palestinian terrorists includes snipers shooting infants, suicide bombers blowing up pizzerias, discos and a university cafeteria, hijackers taking and killing hostages, and infiltrators murdering sleeping families in their homes and Olympic athletes.

- The enemies of Israel rationalize any attacks as legitimate because they do not recognize the right of a Jewish state to exist. Consequently, the Arab bloc and its supporters at the United Nations have succeeded in blocking any condemnation of any terrorist attacks against Israel.

- Islamic Jihad, Hamas, and the PFLP are on the U.S. list of terrorist organizations because their actions satisfy the government's definition of terrorism as "the unlawful use of force or violence against persons or property to intimidate or coerce a government, the civilian population, or any segment thereof, in furtherance of political or social objectives."

HISTORY:

In a July 2002 report, Amnesty International rebutted the suggestion that Palestinian terrorists could be considered "freedom fighters." AI said "attacks on civilians are not permitted under any internationally recognized standard of law, whether they are committed in the context of a struggle against military occupation or any other context. Not only are they considered murder under general principles of law in every national legal system, they are contrary to fundamental principles of humanity which are reflected in international humanitarian law. In the manner in which they are being committed in Israel and the Occupied Territories, they also amount to crimes against humanity."

STATEMENT:

"Arab and Islamic leaders condemn terrorism and responded to President Bush's call to fight terrorism."

ONE FOOT RESPONSES:

- President Bush called on the Arab states to "do everything possible to stop terrorist activities, to disrupt terrorist financing and stop incitement of violence in state-owned media." He also urged them to denounce publicly suicide bombings, and to use their influence with the Palestinian Authority and other groups to stop the violence. Not only did the Arab leaders reject the President's request, they did the exact opposite by further supporting Palestinian terror.

- Many Arab states actively support terrorism. For example, Iraqi President Saddam Hussein publicly promised to pay $25,000 to the families of suicide bombers. Saudi Arabia held a terror telethon to raise millions of dollars for "martyrs" and was the home of most of the September 11 hijackers. Iran ships arms to terrorists in the Palestinian Authority and to Hizballah in Lebanon. Syria also supports Hizballah and serves as headquarters for a number of Palestinian terrorist groups.

- The Organization of the Islamic Conference meeting in Malaysia in 2002 rejected any linkage between Palestinian attacks and terrorism and refused to even define terrorism. Malaysian Prime Minister Mahathir Mohamad called on the group to classify all attacks on civilians, including those by Palestinian suicide bombers, as terrorism, but the Conference would not do so.

HISTORY:

So long as the Arab states continue to support terrorism, Israel will remain at risk, and there is little hope for regional peace or stability. Furthermore, the Arab policy legitimates the use of terror not only against Israel, but other nations as well, including the United States. There has been an eerie silence from the European Union and countries all around the world about this issue.

51

SUBJECT: VIOLENCE

STATEMENT:

"Israel uses excessive force against Palestinian demonstrators."

ONE FOOT RESPONSES:

- The number of Palestinian casualties in clashes is regrettable, but it is important to remember that no Palestinian would be in any danger or risk injury if they were not attacking Israelis. No Palestinian has ever been injured at the negotiating table.

- The use of live-fire by the Palestinians has effectively meant that Israeli forces have had to remain at some distance from those initiating the violence. In addition, the threat of force against Israelis has been a threat of lethal force. Both factors have inhibited the use of traditional methods of riot control.

- Faced with an angry, violent mob, Israeli police and soldiers often have no choice but to defend themselves by firing rubber bullets and, in life-threatening situations, live ammunition. Armed Palestinians use hospitals, schools, and the homes of innocents as shields.

HISTORY:

Typically, Israeli troops coming under attack number fewer than 20 while their assailants number in the hundreds and are armed with stones, Molotov cocktails, pistols, assault rifles, machine guns, hand grenades and explosives. Moreover, mixed among rock throwers have been Palestinians, often policemen, armed with guns. Israel would have no need to use force of any kind if it were not under attack. And even when provoked, Israel usually takes extraordinary precautions, and suffers many casualties, to avoid injuring Palestinian civilians.

STATEMENT:

"Israel's assassinations of Palestinian 'activists' are war crimes— illegal and immoral."

ONE FOOT RESPONSES:

- Assassinations of terrorists are not unprecedented. In 1986, after Libya directed a terrorist bombing that killed one American and injured 200 others, the U.S. tried to assassinate President Muammar Qaddafi. In 1998, the Clinton administration tried to assassinate Osama bin Laden for his role in bombing the U.S. embassies in Tanzania and Kenya.

- Individuals who directly take part in hostilities cannot then claim immunity from attack or protection as innocent civilians. A terrorist who plans bombings and ambushes, is considered a combatant until hostilities come to an end, and is therefore a legitimate military target.

- Assassinations tell terrorists that if they target others, they will become targets themselves. They are pre-emptive strikes at people who would otherwise murder Jews. They throw the terrorists off balance and prevent attacks. By killing terrorist leaders, many lives are saved. Israel prefers to arrest terrorists, but if it can't, and the Palestinians won't, then Israelis have no other choice but to defend themselves.

HISTORY:

Israel is faced with a nearly impossible situation in attempting to protect its civilian population from Palestinians who are prepared to blow themselves up to murder innocents. Israel's preferred strategy for dealing with the problem has been the peace process, but the Palestinians have refused to make political concessions and chosen to use violence to force Israel to capitulate to all their demands. Some critics argue that Israel's policy perpetuates a cycle of violence, but this assumes the terror would stop if Israel didn't respond. The people who blow themselves up to become martyrs, however, are already intent on bombing the Jews out of the Middle East and will not stop until their goal is achieved.

STATEMENT:

"The Israeli army massacred civilians in Jenin in April 2002."

ONE FOOT RESPONSES:

- Secretary of State Colin Powell, Human Rights Watch, the European Union, and the UN all investigated Palestinian claims that Israel was guilty of atrocities in Jenin and concluded the charges were false.

- Jenin is known even by the Palestinians as the "suiciders' capital" and was the source of 28 suicide bombings during the "al-Aksa intifada." Israel did not attack the camp indiscriminately, troops attacked terrorist hideouts. The Palestinians' own review committee subsequently reported that most of the victims were combatants.

- Israel could have used the strategy employed by the U.S. in Afghanistan

and bombed the camp, but the IDF chose the riskier tactic of sending soldiers house to house to reduce the likelihood of endangering civilians. Palestinian terrorists used bombs, booby-traps, and machine guns to turn the camp into a war zone and killed 23 Israeli soldiers. Some civilians were killed because terrorists used them as shields, and much of the damage in the camp was attributable to the terrorists' munitions.

HISTORY:

Like any democracy, Israel has a right and a moral obligation to defend its citizens. Israel wants peace and is prepared to accept a Palestinian state — once the Palestinians recognize Israel's right to exist with their actions, and not just their words. Israel agreed to a U.S.-brokered cease-fire in the hope the Palestinians would do the same and return to the bargaining table, but Yasser Arafat rejected the American plan and the terrorists from Jenin escalated their violent attacks. After suicide bombers terrorized the civilian population for 18 months, Israeli forces had to raid Jenin to root out one of the principal terrorist bases.

STATEMENT:

"Suicide bombers are morally equivalent to the IDF, both of which kill innocent civilians."

ONE FOOT RESPONSES:

- Israeli soldiers and civilians have faced thousands of organized, violent and life-threatening attacks by Palestinians, including violent riots, lynchings, machine-gun fire directed at residential neighborhoods, fire-bombings, roadside charges and ambushes, mortar barrages, suicide bombers and car bombs in crowded shopping areas.

- The IDF targets only terrorists planning acts of violence, and has done its utmost to prevent harm to innocent civilians. When tragic mistakes are made, Israel investigates and apologizes.

- Most Palestinian civilians are hurt participating in violent confrontations; few noncombatants are injured from Israeli attacks on terrorist targets. In contrast, Palestinian roadside bombs have killed and maimed

children in school buses, Israeli children have been stoned to death while hiking, and an infant was shot by a sniper. Suicide bombers have targeted Israelis at malls, restaurants, bus stops, discos, and even a university cafeteria. About 70% of the Israelis killed by terrorists are civilians.

HISTORY:

Palestinian terrorists first began targeting Jews in the early part of the 20th century, long before Israel captured the West Bank and Gaza Strip. Since 1967, the level of terrorism has escalated, and Islamic radicals have adopted the barbaric practice of suicide bombings. To fight against this new tactic, as well as the old proven methods of terrorism, Israel must take defensive measures that sometimes, inadvertently, lead to civilian casualties. There is no moral equivalency, however, between terrorists who knowingly target innocent men, women, and children, and the IDF, which aims for terrorists. The IDF acts with restraint, trying to minimize civilian casualties, while Palestinian suicide bombers murder indiscriminately with the goal of killing as many innocent people as possible.

STATEMENT:

"Both Arafat and Sharon are extremists who are perpetuating the cycle of violence."

ONE FOOT RESPONSES:

- It was Ariel Sharon who advised Prime Minister Begin to dismantle Israeli settlements in the Sinai that made the Israel-Egypt Peace Treaty possible. As Prime Minister, Sharon endorsed the idea of a negotiated Palestinian state and has repeatedly offered to negotiate with the Palestinians if they end the violence. Arafat, in contrast, has a history of sponsoring terrorism. After rejecting the Palestinian state offered by Prime Minister Barak, Arafat instigated a wave of violence.

- Sharon has shown a willingness to seek peace, but Arafat has not. Sharon repeatedly accepted cease-fires and acted with restraint in response to Palestinian terrorism. Arafat consistently violated the cease-fires and instigated new attacks.

- The term "cycle of violence" is misleading. The Palestinians have been targeting innocent civilians. The Israeli army has acted to defend its citizens, arresting or killing known terrorists who Arafat has refused to arrest. Equating terror and counterterror is morally indefensible, akin to comparing an arsonist who sets a fire with the firefighter who tries to put it out

HISTORY:

Sharon was once adamantly opposed to a Palestinian state, but now has openly endorsed the idea of such a state living in peace beside Israel. Arafat has never given up his commitment to create a Palestinian state to replace Israel. Organizations such as Fatah and Force 17, which are under Arafat's direct control, are perpetrating terror attacks. Israel has sought to stop the violence to pursue peace negotiations while Arafat has used terror to scuttle peace talks.

UNITED NATIONS

What creates fundamentalism? "(It) is never rooted in faith but in doubt. It is when we are not sure that we are doubly sure. Fundamentalism is, therefore, inevitable in an age which has destroyed so many certainties…"

Reinhold Neibuhr

The extremist is not a knight of faith; the extremist is a coward in the face of doubt.   (D.W.)

SUBJECT: UNITED NATIONS

STATEMENT:

"The United Nations unjustly partitioned Palestine."

ONE FOOT RESPONSES:

- In 1947, the UN sent a delegation to Palestine that concluded what had long been apparent: The conflicting national aspirations of Jews and Arabs could not be reconciled. When they returned, the majority recommended the establishment of two separate states, Jewish and Arab, with Jerusalem an internationalized enclave.

- The UN General Assembly rejected the Arab demand for a unitary Arab state. The majority recommendation for partition was subsequently adopted 33-13 with 10 abstentions on November 29, 1947.

• The Jews of Palestine were not satisfied with the small territory allotted to them by the UN, nor were they happy that Jerusalem was severed from the Jewish State; nevertheless, they welcomed the compromise. The Arabs rejected it.

HISTORY:

As World War II ended, the magnitude of the Holocaust became known. This accelerated demands for a resolution to the question of Palestine so the survivors of Hitler's "Final Solution" might find sanctuary in a homeland of their own. The British tried to work out an agreement acceptable to both Arabs and Jews, but their insistence on the Arabs' approval guaranteed failure because the Arabs would not make any concessions. They subsequently turned the issue over to the UN in February 1947. As the internationally recognized authority, the UN was empowered to make a decision on how to resolve the issue, as it also did in the partition decision for India and Pakistan the same year. The Arabs were willing to accept the UN decision so long as it was in their favor.

58

STATEMENT:

"UN Resolution 242 requires Israel to return all the land it won in 1967 to the Palestinians."

ONE FOOT RESPONSES:

- The resolution calls for the "Withdrawal of Israeli armed forces from territories occupied in the recent conflict." The UN specifically rejected Arab demands that Israel be required to withdraw from "all the" territories because the Security Council recognized the 1967 borders were indefensible and would have to be adjusted.

- The resolution refers to the "inadmissability of the acquisition of territory by war"; however, this only applies to an offensive war. Otherwise, if a defender had to return all the land it gained, this would encourage aggression, since the aggressor would have nothing to lose by going to war. The ultimate goal of 242 is a "peaceful and accepted settlement." This means a negotiated agreement based on the resolution's principles.

- Israel accepted 242 and has withdrawn from roughly 93% of the territories it captured in 1967. It signed peace treaties with every Arab state that has truly recognized its right to exist, namely, Egypt and Jordan.

HISTORY:

Resolution 242 was written to establish principles to guide negotiations for an Arab-Israeli peace settlement. Israel has already proven itself and followed those principles in negotiations with other countries. The Palestinians are not mentioned and nowhere does it require that Palestinians be given any political rights or territory. The resolution does call for "termination of all claims or states of belligerency" and the recognition that "every State in the area" has the "right to live in peace within secure and recognized boundaries free from threats or acts of force."

STATEMENT:

"The UN has played a balanced role in Middle East affairs."

ONE FOOT RESPONSES:

- Starting in the mid-1970s, an Arab-Soviet-Third World bloc joined to form what amounted to a pro-Palestinian lobby at the UN. A pro-PLO "Committee on the Inalienable Rights of the Palestinian People" was established in 1975, the same year the General Assembly branded Zionism as racism. While Israel's actions are routinely condemned by the UN, no terrorist attack or other hostile action toward Israel ever merits a critical resolution.

- Israel is the object of more investigative committees and special representatives than any other state in the UN system. The Commission on Human Rights routinely adopts totally disproportionate resolutions concerning Israel while rogue states such as Syria and Libya are never criticized.

- The Palestinians have been afforded special treatment at the UN since 1975 when the General Assembly awarded the PLO permanent representative status. In 1988, the PLO was designated as "Palestine" and, later, the Palestinians were given the unique status of non-voting member of the Assembly. In contrast, Israel was until 2002 the only UN member state ineligible to sit on the Security Council (and even that right is temporary) and remains barred from other key UN bodies.

HISTORY:

The United States does not automatically support Israel with its veto in the UN Security Council. The U.S. has often opposed Israel in the Council and has rarely used its veto. The Bush Administration announced a change in policy in 2002, declaring that it would veto any resolution that didn't condemn Palestinian terror and name Hamas, Islamic Jihad, and the Al-Aksa Martyrs Brigade as the groups responsible for the attacks. The U.S. also said that resolutions must note that any Israeli withdrawal is linked to the security situation, and that both parties must be called upon to pursue a negotiated settlement. Nevertheless, the U.S. abstained on the very next unbalanced resolution criticizing Israel.

60

MAPS

"The opposite of love is not hate but indifference; the opposite of life is not death but insensitivity."—Elie Wiesel from *Somewhere a Master: Further Hasidic Portraits and Legends*.

Elie Wiesel, a survivor of Auschwitz who ever calls us to conscience, indicates that **caring** matters most of all. Apathy causes more harm than even hatred because the energy that comes from strong feelings can ultimately lead to reconciliation. But no improvements can come from indifference and insensitivity.   (L.L.)

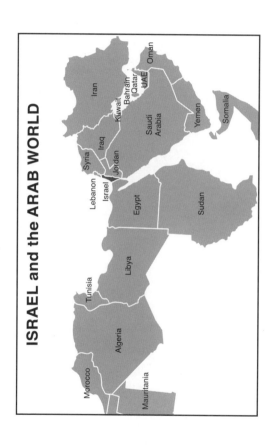

ISRAEL and the ARAB WORLD

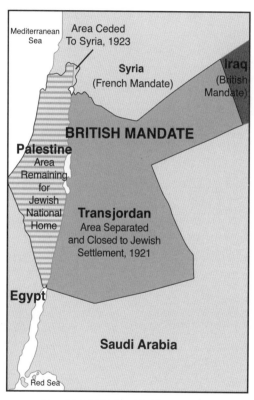

Great Britain's Division of the Mandated Area

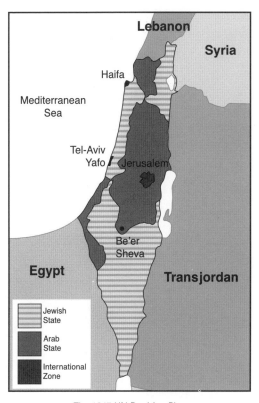

The 1947 UN Partition Plan

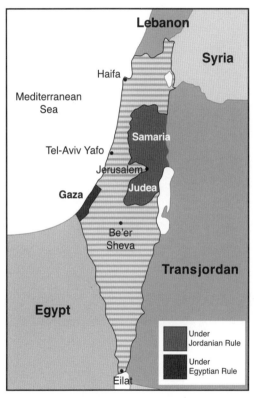

Israel Before June 1967

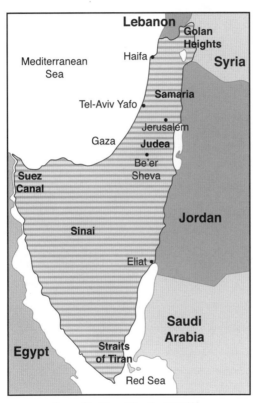

Cease-Fire Lines After the 1967 War

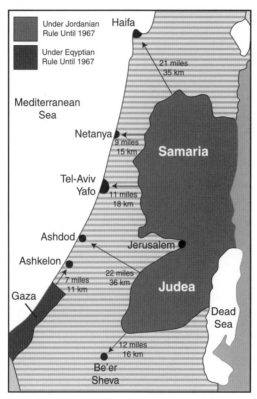

Distances Between Israeli Population Centers
and Pre-1967 Armistice Lines.

BIBLIOGRAPHY

On his deathbed, Reb Zusya began to cry. His disciples, gathered around, asked in astonishment: Rabbi, why do you cry? You have been a great teacher and a pious man!" Reb Zusya replied, "When I come before God, I know he will not ask me – why have you not been faithful as Abraham. For I have not the towering strength of an Abraham. He will not ask me, "Why were you not a leader like Moses?" For I have not the spiritual stature of Moses. But when God says to me "Zusya, my child – why were you not Zusya?", then what shall I say? That is why I cry.

Chasidic Story   (D.W.)

BIBLIOGRAPHY

Aumann, Moshe. *Land Ownership in Palestine 1880-1948.* Jerusalem: Academic Committee on the Middle East, 1976.

Avineri, Shlomo. *The Making of Modern Zionism: Intellectual Origins of the Jewish State.* N.Y.: Basic Books, 1981.

Avneri, Arieh. *The Claim of Dispossession.* N.J.: Transaction Publishers, 1984.

Bard, Mitchell and Moshe Schwartz. *1001 Facts Everyone Should Know About Israel.* N.J.: Jason Aronson, 2002.

Bard, Mitchell G. *From Tragedy to Triumph: The Politics behind the Rescue of Ethiopian Jewry.* Conn.: Greenwood, 2002.

Bard, Mitchell G. *Myths and Facts: A Guide to the Arab-Israeli Conflict.* Md.: AICE, 2002.

Bard, Mitchell G. *The Water's Edge and Beyond.* N.J.: Transaction Publishers, 1991.

Becker, Jillian. *The PLO.* N.Y.: St. Martin's Press, 1985.

Begin, Menachem. *The Revolt.* N.Y.: EP Dutton, 1978.

Bell, J. Bowyer. *Terror Out of Zion.* N.J.: Transaction Publishers, 1996.

Ben-Gurion, David. *Rebirth and Destiny of Israel.* N.Y.: Philosophical Library, 1954.

Benvenisti, Meron. *City of Stone: The Hidden History of Jerusalem.* Calif.: University of California Press, 1996.

Cohen, Aharon. *Israel and the Arab World.* N.Y.: Funk and Wagnalls, 1970.

Collins, Larry, and Dominique Lapierre. *O Jerusalem!* N.Y.: Simon and Schuster, 1972.

Dimont, Max. *Jews, God and History.* N.Y.: Mentor Books, 1994.

BIBLIOGRAPHY

Eban, Abba. *Heritage: Civilization and the Jews.* N.Y.: Summit Books, 1984.

Gilbert, Martin. *Israel: A History.* N.Y.: William Morrow & Co., 1998.

Goitein, S.D. *Jews and Arabs.* N.Y.: Schocken Books, 1974.

Hazony, Yoram. *The Jewish State: The Struggle for Israel's Soul.* N.Y.: Basic Books, 2001.

Hertzberg, Arthur. *The Zionist Idea.* Philadelphia: The Jewish Publication Society, 1997.

Herzl, Theodor. *The Jewish State.* Dover Publications, 1989.

Herzog, Chaim. *The Arab-Israeli Wars.* N.Y.: Random House, 1984.

Hourani, Albert. *A History of the Arab Peoples.* N.Y.: Warner Books, 1992.

Jabotinsky, Z'ev. *The War and the Jew.* N.Y.: Altalena Press, 1987.

Johnson, Paul. *A History of the Jews.* N.Y.: HarperCollins, 1988.

Katz, Samuel. *Battleground: Fact and Fantasy in Palestine.* SPI Books, 1986.

Kollek, Teddy. *Jerusalem.* Washington, D.C.: Washington Institute For Near East Policy, 1990.

Laqueur, Walter. *A History of Zionism.* Fine Communications, 1997.

Laqueur, Walter, and Barry Rubin. *The Israel-Arab Reader.* N.Y.: Penguin, 2001.

Lenczowski, George. *The Middle East in World Affairs.* N.Y.: Cornell University Press, 1980.

Lewis, Bernard. *Islam and the West.* N.Y.: Oxford University Press, 1994.

BIBLIOGRAPHY

Lewis, Bernard. *The Jews of Islam*. N.Y.: Princeton University Press, 2002.

Lewis, Bernard. *The Middle East: A Brief History of the Last 2000 Years*. N.Y.: Touchstone Books, 1997.

Livingstone, Neil C., and David Halevy. *Inside the PLO*. N.Y.: William Morrow and Co., 1990.

Lorch, Netanel. *One Long War*. N.Y.: Herzl Press, 1976.

Lukacs, Yehuda. *Israel, Jordan, and the Peace Process*. Syracuse, N.Y.: Syracuse University Press, 1997.

Meir, Golda. *My Life*. N.Y.: Dell, 1975.

Netanyahu, Benjamin. *A Place Among the Nations: Israel and the World*. N.Y.: Warner Books, 1998.

Oren, Michael. *Six Days of War: June 1967 and the Making of the Modern Middle East*. N.Y.: Oxford University Press, 2002.

Pipes, Daniel. *In the Path of God: Islam and Political Power*. N.Y.: Basic Books, 1983.

Porath, Yehoshua. *The Emergence of the Palestinian-Arab National Movement, 1918-1929*. London: Frank Cass, 1996.

Porath, Yehoshua. *In Search of Arab Unity 1930-1945*. London: Frank Cass and Co., Ltd., 1986.

Porath, Yehoshua. *Palestinian Arab National Movement: From Riots to Rebellion: 1929-1939*. Vol. 2. London: Frank Cass and Co., Ltd., 1977.

Quandt, William B. *Camp David: Peacemaking and Politics*. Washington, D.C.: Brookings Institution, 1986.

BIBLIOGRAPHY

Rabin, Yitzhak. *The Rabin Memoirs.* Calif.: University of California Press, 1996.

Rubenstein, Amnon. *The Zionist Dream Revisited: From Herzl to Gush Emunim and Back.* N.Y.: Schocken Books, 1987.

Sachar, Abram Leon. *History of the Jews.* N.Y.: Random House, 1982.

Sachar, Howard. *A History of Israel: From the Rise of Zionism to Our Time.* N.Y.: Alfred A. Knopf, 1998.

Safran, Nadav. *Israel: The Embattled Ally.* Cambridge: Harvard University Press, 1981.

Schiff, Ze'Ev, and Ehud Ya'ari. *Intifada.* N.Y.: Simon & Schuster, 1990.

Schiff, Ze'Ev, and Ehud Ya'ari. *Israel's Lebanon War.* N.Y.: Simon and Schuster, 1984.

Spiegel, Steven. *The Other Arab-Israeli Conflict: Making America's Middle East Policy from Truman to Reagan.* IL: University of Chicago Press, 1986.

Stillman, Norman. *The Jews of Arab Lands.* Philadelphia: Jewish Publication Society, 1989.

Stillman, Norman. *The Jews of Arab Lands in Modern Times.* Philadelphia: Jewish Publication Society, 1991.

Weizmann, Chaim. *Trial and Error.* N.Y.: Greenwood Press, 1972.

Ye'or, Bat. *The Dhimmi.* N.J.: Associated University Press, 1985.

WEB-OGRAPHY

We live and act according to the image of humanity we cherish.

—*Abraham Joshua Heschel*

If we imagine that the human heart is bent solely on evil and that human nature is fundamentally corrupt, then we will find the devil wherever we look. If, on the other hand, we have more faith in our species, grant ourselves a basic instinct toward altruism and fairness, we might very well decide that decent people make up the majority of our race. It all depends upon whom we greet each morning in the mirror.   (E.F.)

ISRAEL

Begin-Sadat Center for
  Strategic Studies . . . . www.biu.ac.il/SOC/besa

Central Zionist Archives. . . . . www.wzo.org.il/cza/index.htm

Golan Heights Information Server . . . . . http://english.golan.org.il

Institute for Advanced Strategic
  and Political Studies . . . . www.iasps.org.il

Israel Defense Forces (IDF). . . . . www.idf.il

Israeli Central
  Bureau of Statistics. . . . . www.cbs.gov.il/engindex.htm

Israeli Ministry of
  Foreign Affairs . . . . www.mfa.gov.il

Israeli Prime Minister's Office . . . . www.pmo.gov.il/english

Jaffee Center for Strategic Studies . . . . www.tau.ac.il/jcss

Jerusalem Center for Public Affairs . . . . www.jcpa.org

Jewish Virtual Library. . . . . www.JewishVirtualLibrary.org

The Knesset - The Israeli Parliament . . . . www.knesset.gov.il

MEMRI. . . . . www.memri.org

Peace Now. . . . . www.peace-now.org

The Peres Center for Peace . . . . www.peres-center.co.il

World Zionist Organization Student
  and Academics Department . . . . www.wzo.org.il

The Yesha Council of Judea
  Samaria and Gaza . . . . www.moetzetyesha.co.il

TERRORISM

International Policy Institute
for Counter-Terrorism . . . . www.ict.org.il

Terrorism-Counter-
Terrorism Page . . . . www.emergency.com/cntrterr.htm

The Terrorism
Research Center . . . . www.terrorism.com/welcome.htm

U.S. State Department Office of Counterterrorism
. . . . www.state.gov/www/global/terrorism/index.html

U.S.-ISRAEL RELATIONS

American Israel Public Affairs
Committee (AIPAC) . . . . www.aipac.org

American-Israeli Cooperative
Enterprise (AICE) . . . . www.jewishvirtuallibrary.org

American Jewish Committee . . . . www.ajc.org

Anti-Defamation League (ADL). . . . . www.adl.org

B'nai B'rith . . . . http://bnaibrith.org

Jewish National Fund (JNF) . . . . www.jnf.org

Jewish Institute for National
Security Affairs (JINSA) . . . . www.jinsa.org

United Jewish Communities: The
Federations of North America. . . . . www.ujc.org

The Washington Institute
for Near East Policy . . . . www.washingtoninstitute.org

World Jewish Congress (WJC). . . . . www.wjc.org.il